Music for Flute & Piano

Volume 3

CONTENTS

To access audio visit:
www.halleonard.com/mylibrary

Enter Code
7739-4336-0568-4933

ISBN 978-1-59615-308-0

MMO Music Minus One

EXCLUSIVELY DISTRIBUTED BY

HAL•LEONARD®
7777 W. BLUEMOUND RD. P.O. BOX 13819 MILWAUKEE, WI 53213

Visit Hal Leonard Online at
www.halleonard.com

PERFORMANCE GUIDE
COMMENTARY BY DORIOT ANTHONY DWYER

WALTER PISTON
Sonata

This piece was composed by Walter Piston for Georges Laurent, my predecessor in the Boston Symphony, in 1930.

In the first movement, the piano part has quite a different texture from the flute part. The piano part opens in a very quiet and active way. It is rather spooky and bland, a series of unaccented, unshaped equal notes. It is therefore the flute which gives the movement its shape. I like to think of it as a barcarolle. The nineteenth century composer Jacques Offenbach wrote the most famous barcarolle, but this twentieth century version is quite different from its predecessor! The similarity is in the rhythmic propulsion.

The subject after the *poco meno allegro* (measures 42 to 44) should not be hurried, but should nevertheless be very jaunty. The *tempo primo* that follows in measure 63, where the flute has a figure similar to the opening passages of the piano, should be comparable to the piano in mood—very even and soft. After the piano comes in at bar 74 with its theme reminiscent of the flute part, the climactic section begins. In the accelerando at the end, I suggest that you do not play at your maximum speed, but sound as if you are doing so. Be sure to play bar 164 very softly so that the last bar will be a big surprise.

The second movement recorded here is a highly abridged version of the longer, original second movement. Do look into the entire movement, as there are some very beautiful singing parts in it. Again, in the second movement, the piano texture is somewhat different from the flute texture, although the two instruments do exchange parts.

Pause between the second and third movements, starting the third as the overtones from the second die away. This means that the third movement must start softly to match those dying overtones. Play the first note *pianissimo,* making a slight crescendo on the second and third eighth notes so that the dynamic level reaches *piano.* Keep the sound in the distance until the crescendo indicated six bars later.

The second theme of the third movement has a character similar to that of the first movement, which is quite typical of Piston. On the repeated D's, if you phrase in four-bar sections you will find the passage easier than if you were to play each bar as a separate entity. In spite of the diminuendo in bar 87, give the impression of a *subito piano;* Mr. Piston desires a marked drop in dynamic level. If you make a slight pause, as if you were going to breathe, before the *piano,* it somehow "clears the air."

HENRI DUTILLEUX
Sonatine

This work was written as a contest piece for the Paris Conservatory and is dedicated to Professor Gaston Crunelle of that school.

Mr. Dutilleux commented to me that the theme should flow and move. Although he apologized for his piano playing, I found it very elegant, particularly at the Animée before number 8. At number 7, also, the marking is *animée;* be sure that you do not get faster too early. Before 11, Mr. Dutilleux did not want the triplets observed religiously. And at the end of the piece, do not ritard even though this is a great temptation. In other words, one must judge which instructions the composer means literally and which he means in the spirit of the piece. Generally, this spirit can be discovered by looking at both the flute and piano parts and considering melody, harmony, and rhythm simultaneously.

I would like to bring to your attention a passage that is of special pleasure to Mr. Dutilleux and to me, too. Between 13 and 14, there is a *pianissimo* on a high A. This is one very typical characteristic of Dutilleux, a change in texture. It is not so much that this note should be very soft, although that helps, but it should be different from the preceding six bars. Six bars before the *pianissimo,* on the C trill, the piano begins a rather plunky theme. It is jumpy, like throwing stones in the water. Where it says *pianissimo,* you should change your texture to something diatonic and diaphonous, more on the horizontal plane.

There are many places where the texture changes. Generally, this is where the flute part is marked *piano.* You want to make sure that the background and the feeling of the soloist react to the textural change. For instance, at number 2, where the piano starts out on its jaunty theme, there is a change from what the flute was doing three bars before. There should be a change of mood as well as of texture. Five bars before 4, there is an imitative passage between flute and piano. Even though it is in 6/8, it sounds as if in waltz time. It is very pulsated and repetitious, becoming more and more animated through the trill. Then, at 4, the harmony of the piano drops down to the bass, and should be executed in a startling manner.

Doriot Anthony Dwyer

MMO 8107

SONATA

Walter Piston

I

MMO 8107

4

6

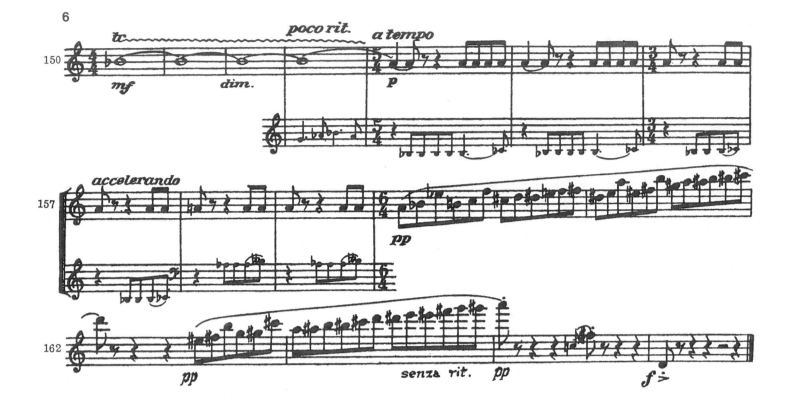

II

optional cut to measure 37

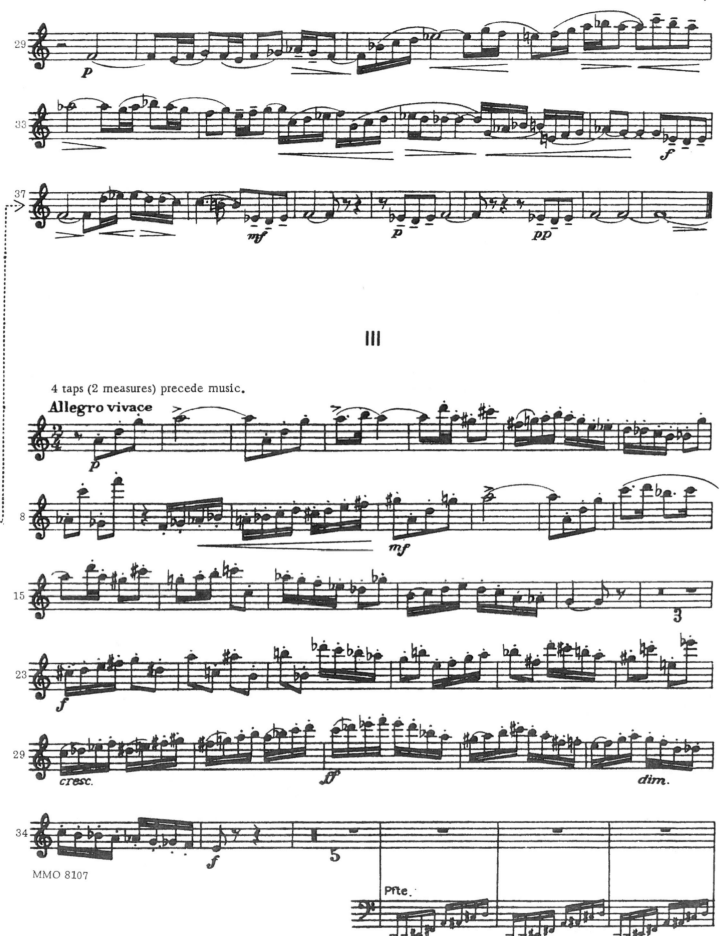

III

4 taps (2 measures) precede music.

Allegro vivace

9

MMO 8107

SONATINE

Henri Dutilleux

12

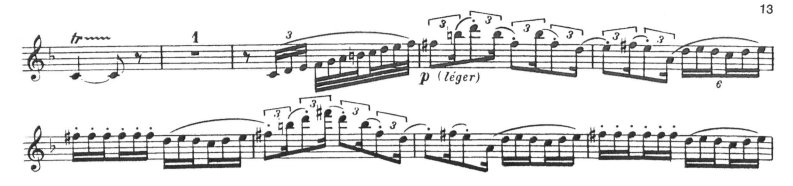

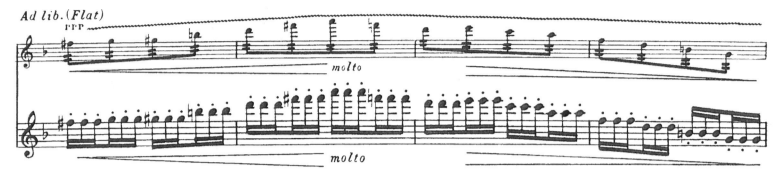

14

peu   à   peu

16 Reprenez   le   mouvement   peu   à

pp *(mysterieux)*

peu   Animez

progressivement

17

Animez   toùjours   jusqu'à   la   fin   *sfz*   *sfz*

sfz   *sfz*

ff

MMO 8107